American Archaeology

UNCOVERS THE WESTWARD MOVEMENT

LOIS MINER HUEY

 **Marshall Cavendish**
Benchmark
New York

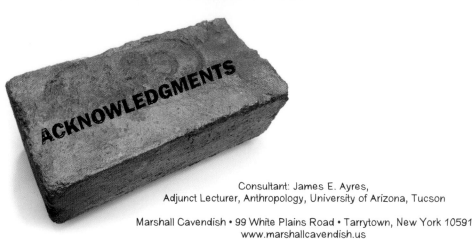

ACKNOWLEDGMENTS

Consultant: James E. Ayres,
Adjunct Lecturer, Anthropology, University of Arizona, Tucson

Marshall Cavendish • 99 White Plains Road • Tarrytown, New York 10591
www.marshallcavendish.us

Library of Congress Cataloging–in–Publication Data
Huey, Lois Miner.
American archaeology uncovers the westward movement / by Lois Miner Huey.
p. cm.— (American archaeology) Includes bibliographical references and index.
ISBN 978–0–7614–4265–3
1. United States—Territorial expansion—Juvenile literature. 2. West (U.S.)—History—Juvenile literature.
3. Frontier and pioneer life—West (U.S.)—Juvenile literature. 4. Historical geography—United States—
Juvenile literature. 5. Archaeology and history—West (U.S.)—Juvenile literature.
6. Excavations (Archaeology)—West (U.S.)—Juvenile literature. I. Title.
E179.5.H847 2010
978'.01—dc22

2009003167

Photo research by: Tracey Engel
Cover photo, top: Students conduct a dig at a university's science camp.

Artifacts at bottom: left, slate fragment with an incised design, found at a fort on the Santa Fe Trail; center,
broken ceramics, found at the same Santa Fe fort; right, a horseshoe excavated at Coronado's camp.

Front cover: AP Images/Bob Child (top); Courtesy of the National Park Service (bottom, left; bottom, center);
Deni Seymour (bottom, right); iStock © Vishnu Mulakala, back cover; iStock © Alex Nikado
Title page: iStock © Lisa Thorinberg, iStock © Vishnu Mulakala

The photographs in this book are used by permission and through the courtesy of:
AP Images: Bob Child, 4; Utah Historical Society, 31. Corbis: George H. H. Huey, 18–19; 20; Lowell Georgia,
41; James L. Amos, 52–53. Getty Images: Hulton Archive, 9, 12–13, 26; James L. Amos/National Geographic,
28–29, 36–37. The Granger Collection, New York: 30, 46–47. Courtesy of the National Park Service:
23, 24, 25, 43, 44, 45; Fonda Thomson, 50. Printed with permission of the New York State Museum,
Albany, NY, 12230: 5 (bottom). Bob Neyland: 35. Julie M. Schablitsky: 33. Photographed by Deni J.
Seymour;artifacts curated at the Floyd County Historical Museum: 16, 17 (both). 3; iStock © Eric Isselee,
iStock © Kals Tomats, 4; iStock © ObservePhoto, 5; Shutterstock © Najin, 6; iStock © Richard Goerg, iStock ©
Richard Cano, 7; iStock © Alex Nikado, 14; Shutterstock © Biuliq, iStock © Emrah Oztas, iStock © Jens Stolt, 26;
iStock © Torsten Lorenz

Printed in Malaysia
135642

CONTENTS

WHAT IS Historical Archaeology?

Archaeologists dig into the ground to find food bones, building remains, and tools used by people in the past. Historical archaeologists are looking for clues about what happened in America after Europeans arrived.

A group of students at the "Kids Are Scientists, Too" camp conduct an archaeological investigation at the former site of an eighteenth-century home on the University of Connecticut campus at Storrs.

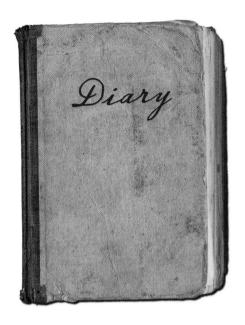

Yes, written documents tell some of the story. Historical archaeologists research documents like maps, diaries, land deeds, and letters to help understand what happened on a site. But those documents do not usually talk about regular people, the ones who did not write letters or diaries. Historical archaeologists are especially interested in learning about the lives of servants, poor farmers, and soldiers who built America.

How do archaeologists do this? By studying people's garbage.

What folks used and threw away tells more about their daily lives than objects kept on shelves out of harm's way. Archaeologists want to study the stuff that did not make it into museums—objects that were broken and discarded after much use. The garbage.

Broken dishes and glassware tell archaeologists what people of the past chose for setting their tables. Studying the bones of people's food, as well as their butchering techniques, provides information about what people ate and how they cooked. When archaeologists measure uncovered house and barn foundations, they find out how people crafted buildings, what size and shape they were, and how they were used. Buttons, straight pins, gun parts, and toys are clues to how people dressed, defended their homes, and spent their leisure time.

How do historical archaeologists know they are collecting information about people who lived in the 1600s rather than people from the 1800s? They use a method called stratigraphy (struh-TIG-ra-fee). Over time, layers of soil called strata build up on a site through natural causes or when people add their own materials. By carefully scraping away the soil with small tools, archaeologists dig down through time. They begin with upper levels of soil, in which they may find nineteenth-century layers. As they work their way down, they reach eighteenth-century layers, seventeenth-century layers, and so on. In some areas, the layers go back as far as Viking times. Prehistoric Native American layers are often found at the deepest level. The scientists dig each layer separately and collect its artifacts. Once the uppermost layer has been removed, the archaeologists have dug through the lives of everyone who lived on that site at a given time.

Based on what they find, archaeologists interpret the artifacts from each time period to understand how people's lives changed. *Change* is a big word in archaeology. How people lived—and how and when that changed— is an important part of the interpretation. As new evidence appears, archaeologists sometimes have to change their interpretations. That makes archaeology really interesting.

Stratigraphy is the key to understanding the past. Sticking a shovel straight down into the ground and pulling up the soil would disturb the stratigraphy, mix up the layers, and mix up the time periods. Archaeologists use shovel testing only to find a site. Then they switch over to small tools and painstakingly remove the layers one by one.

As archaeologists study a site, they carefully draw, map, and photograph building remains. Artifacts are taken back to the lab, where workers wash and store them. Codes are written on each object so that it is clear exactly where the artifact was found. Scientists run tests on charcoal, soil, and remains found inside bottles. Then the archaeologist writes up the results of the research so everyone can know what was learned. Museum displays often follow.

The world which we think of as ours was thought by people in the past to be theirs. Our knowledge of everyday events in the lives of people who lived long ago seems to be washed away by time. By digging in the ground and studying documents, an archaeologist seems to take a voyage to the distant past in a time machine.

Read about archaeology in books and magazines, go to museums, watch programs on television, and maybe visit a local archaeology dig. Someday you, too, might decide to use the tools of archaeology to study the past.

The Westward Movement

Immigrants to the New World settled, moved on, settled, then moved on again in a restless kind of rhythm, heading north, south, and west. This movement started early and included people from many different places. Travel attempted before about 1850 was especially difficult as people struggled to find easier and safer ways to get to their western destinations.

A nineteenth-century painting by W.J. Jackson, showing the Oregon Trail beyond Devil's Gate, Wyoming. Most wagons going west were pulled by oxen, not horses.

Western trails and roads were made first by those following bison herds or looking for furs. Settlers soon followed until the Santa Fe, Oregon, California, and Mormon trails were well known and well traveled. Why did people go west? Adventure; hopes for a better, freer life; eagerness to get rich quick; escape from the law: there were many reasons.

Although the settlers moved west filled with fear of Indian attack, these fears largely were unfounded or greatly exaggerated. According to one source, along the Oregon and California trails between 1840 and 1860, 362 overlanders and 426 Indians were killed. In 1846 four travelers and twenty Indians died. Most of the conflict came when Indian raiding parties stole cattle or horses. But settlers often lost their lives or were unsuccessful because they knew little about Indians and conditions in the West.

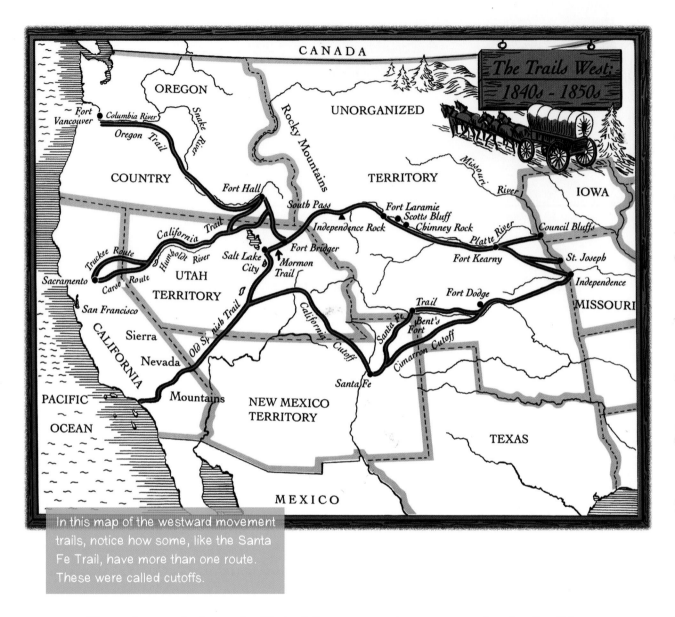

In this map of the westward movement trails, notice how some, like the Santa Fe Trail, have more than one route. These were called cutoffs.

Not only people from the United States went into western lands. So did Mexicans from the South, Russians from the North, Chinese from Asia, and French and English Canadians. Indian tribes in the East were pushed west by white settlers. One author wrote, "the American West . . . was claimed by no less than six different European/American countries. . . ."

A study of the early movements west involves looking at sites associated with many different people. Archaeologists have excavated camps, forts, and trading posts and have searched for early trails, asking what happened to travelers along the way. How did they get where they were going? The discoveries described here focus on early travelers from the 1500s to the middle 1800s, some of whom blazed the trails west or showed that it was possible to make the trek into unknown territory.

One
The Mysterious Coronado Trail

The Spanish explorer Coronado created one trail west in the 1500s. His mission? To find villages in lands north of what is now Mexico that were thought to be full of gold, silver, and precious jewels. He did not find them. After twenty months of wandering through the territory, his Spanish expedition returned home, Coronado himself a victim of severe injuries from falling off his horse. Although his trail was not used later by settlers, he did establish Mexico's claim to much of the West.

In this imaginative nineteenth–century painting by Frederic Remington, members of Coronado's troop are shown crossing the Kansas plains.

Coronado

Francisco Vázquez de Coronado was a nobleman born in Spain in 1510. He came to Mexico at the age of twenty-five as assistant to the Spanish ruler. Within a few years he became governor of an important Mexican province, but he wanted more. During his famous 1540s expedition, he traveled all the way to the Colorado River between California and Arizona, discovered the Grand Canyon, and explored parts of Kansas and New Mexico. Failing to find riches, Coronado returned to Mexico and his job as governor. Eventually he was found guilty of mistreating the Indians and lost his job. He worked for the Mexico City government until his death in 1554.

Where did Coronado's expedition go? This was one of the great mysteries about the early westward movement. Although expedition members kept journals, the names they gave to the Indian settlements they found, called pueblos, were different from the ones used today, so their route is hard to trace. But Coronado's group consisted of more than one thousand Spanish soldiers, women, children, slaves, and Indians. They herded 7,500 head of livestock, including cattle and sheep. How could such a huge crowd not leave more signs on the landscape?

A Coronado Campsite

In the 1980s the first definite remains of a Coronado campsite were found accidentally near Albuquerque, New Mexico. The route for a new modern road had been partially excavated by archaeologists, but they had not dug deep enough. When the grading machine roared to life, it exposed large patches of charcoal stains mixed with pottery more than 2 feet [1 meter] down. After two months of working there, archaeologists knew they had found a Coronado campsite and had learned what one looked like.

The Spanish dug at least fifteen shallow rooms into the ground. Each small room contained many artifacts, some shoveled in to fill the rooms when the camp was abandoned. The rooms had trampled-down clay floors, hearths, burned areas, pits, and postholes. The pits were dug in the floor for storage, while the postholes held upright timber supports for the roof. Hearths were built in the middle of the floor; some along an end wall. In two rooms, shallow depressions along the edge of the hearth pit were shelves used to store "comals," a type of griddle for making tortillas. The firewood in hearths was mostly from pine trees. Apparently the Indians living in a nearby pueblo now called Santiago had already used up the trees in the immediate area. The campsite inhabitants hiked miles, probably to the mountains, to find even this kind of soft wood that was much less satisfactory for burning.

Campsite Clues

Artifacts such as sheep bones and metal tools could have been left only by the Spanish, as these were unknown to Indians at that time. Radiocarbon dates obtained on the corn, bean, and charcoal remains all yielded dates in the mid-1500s, the time Coronado was there.

Metal artifacts included straight pins, nails, part of a hook and eye for fastening clothing, and armor plates worn by soldiers. Food bones and shells showed that the occupants ate sheep, rabbits, turkeys, and bird eggs. But most of the food remains came from wild animals, especially pronghorn and mule deer, so the inhabitants did extensive hunting. Because they were cooked, the animal bones and corn kernels were burned.

Plant food remains included sunflower seeds, corncobs, corn kernels, and beans, probably obtained from the nearby pueblo. Cotton seeds were found in two adjoining rooms. Someone was processing raw cotton, perhaps to squeeze oil from the seeds.

Bolt Heads

In the first half of the 1500s, crossbows were a common Spanish weapon. Wooden arrows with copper heads were fired from the strings of curved wooden frames. The copper "bolt heads" are found on early Spanish battlefields, campsites, and in pueblos where the Spanish stayed. A recent scientific study of these items concentrated on where the metal in the bolt heads came from. Four of the five bolt heads studied contained metal that came from mines in Spain. The fifth probably was made from ore mined in Mexico. Since Mexican mines were not active until after Coronado's expedition, the four made of Spanish metal must have been carried in by his men. This is a valuable tool for distinguishing Coronado sites from later ones.

Excavations in the ruins of the nearby pueblo, Santiago, in the 1930s uncovered European artifacts. These included Spanish-style dishes such as soup plates, a bowl or cup, and a chocolate pitcher. Metal artifacts included a copper knife blade, ammunition (bolt heads) for crossbows, pieces of armor, an iron pitcher handle, and a piece of gold leaf.

Documents indicate that Coronado and his army spent the winters of 1540–1541 and 1541–1542 in the same place. Both winters were so cold that the Spanish laid siege to a nearby pueblo and took Indian homes for themselves. A skeleton found in one room at Santiago with a bolt head in his chest is evidence that the Indians resisted, but lost. Not everyone in Coronado's party could fit in the pueblo, so many camped nearby and dug down into the earth. Those at the campsite probably were mostly Indians and Spanish troops in charge of horses and livestock.

A horseshoe left behind by the Spanish was excavated at the Coronado expedition camp.

Other campsites now have been found, and, with this information, Coronado's trail has been outlined. The exact point of Coronado's entry into what is now the United States remains unclear. Recent discoveries may make that clear.

A horse jangle bridle part found by archaeologists at the Coronado expedition camp

Permanent Spanish settlement did not immediately follow Coronado's expedition, but his two-year trip into the western states established Mexico's claim to all this territory. In the early nineteenth century, when U.S. citizens wanted to settle in what are now California, New Mexico, Arizona, Texas, and even Kansas, they had to get permission from the Mexican government first. Tension between the two governments led to a war with Mexico that ended in 1848 with the United States acquiring much of this land. After that, many people came to settle.

A bolt head left behind by the Spanish. To be hit with this would be devastating.

Radiocarbon Testing

Living things absorb radioactivity. Items such as bone, charcoal produced by burning wood from trees, and seeds are often used for radiocarbon dating. When a living thing dies, the radioactivity begins to decrease through time at a regular, measurable rate. Radiocarbon dating involves testing items such as charcoal from a hearth, for example. By measuring the amount by which the radioactivity has decreased in the charcoal, a scientist can count back in time and arrive at the date when the charcoal was created. These dates then establish the date when the hearth last was used.

Two

An Early Fort on the Santa Fe Trail

The Santa Fe Trail was a route used more by businessmen than settlers. It led from the state of Missouri into Mexico, with its most important stop being the bustling Mexican town of Santa Fe, for which the trail was named.

Remains of the Santa Fe Trail still can be seen, as shown in this photograph.

After resting, resupplying, and trading in Santa Fe, the businessmen went farther into Mexico to obtain more goods to ship back to the United States. American-made goods were hauled along the trail; Mexican and Navaho Indian goods and buffalo robes from Plains Indians were hauled back to Missouri. Trading posts established along the Santa Fe Trail provided places for travelers to rest, resupply, and obtain goods to sell.

Two brothers, Charles and William Bent, along with their partner Ceran Saint Vrain, wanted to make money in the fur trade. Construction of a fort about 1833 in today's state of Colorado along the Arkansas River attracted mountain men and Indians who brought in furs. Bent's Fort—the first of two and therefore called Bent's Old Fort—was an outpost on the very edge of American civilization, right on the border with Mexican territory.

The Southern Cheyenne and the Arapaho were two major Indian tribes that did business at Bent's Old Fort. William Bent maintained good relations with them. He married a Cheyenne woman named Owl Woman, and, when she

Bent's Old Fort National Historic Site, Colorado. The site can be visited year round.

died, he married her sister, Yellow Woman. He helped establish peace between the Cheyenne, Kiowa, and Comanche tribes. After a peace conference called by the Indians in 1840, the groups mixed freely at the fort. When difficulties arose, meetings held at the fort helped resolve problems peacefully. Bent's Old Fort not only provided the usual advantages of a trading post and fort, but it also helped keep the peace for many years.

The fort prospered in the fur trade. Kit Carson, a famous western explorer and trader, sometimes worked for the company. The U.S. Army granted the Bents contracts to supply various exploring expeditions and military troops that moved through. However, with the end of the Mexican War and the discovery of gold in California, the greatly increased flood of troops and travelers down the trail alarmed local Indians. Soon there were more war parties than traders near the fort. Business fell off; in the summer of 1849, William Bent decided to close.

According to stories, William Bent loaded goods in a caravan of wagons and rode away. Later, while the group set up camp, he rode back. He set fire to gunpowder that had been left behind and blew up the fort walls. The fort he built at another location became known as Bent's New Fort.

In the twentieth century, the site of Bent's Old Fort became a Colorado state historic site. Archaeologists located and outlined its walls. In 1963 the National Park Service took over. Three years of archaeological excavations followed, and, based on that work, the fort was reconstructed.

A Fort with Flair

Travelers on the Santa Fe Trail may have thought they already had crossed into Mexico when Bent's Old Fort, built on an open plain, loomed up in front of them. The reddish walls were adobe brick with soft curves and enclosed a large open square. Unlike Mexican structures, however, the fort was two stories high and had round towers at two corners. The glint of sunlight off glass windows would also have suggested this was not a Mexican building, since window glass was rarely used in Mexico until later.

Archaeologists discovered that the round towers were used as storage for military items such as cutlasses and pikes. Numerous whetstones for sharpening these metal weapons were found inside the east tower. Also found there were ox-yoke pins, meat hooks, and parts of a powder flask. Inside the west tower were the remains of a burned wagon. The west tower, unlike what documents and maps show, was larger than the east one.

A corral built inside the fort rather than outside the walls was another unusual feature. It was triangular, lined inside with clay, and surrounded by posts. The noise and smell of the animals must have been a constant fact of life for the inhabitants!

Archaeologists found evidence that temporary structures such as lean-tos were used by the fort's builders. Large pits were dug out for clay to make adobe brick, and the fort's houses and stores were built over the pits. The quality of the adobe bricks was poor, but with frequent maintenance, the bricks served their purpose for the twenty years the fort stood.

Go to Your Room!

Doors into the rooms were opened by turning brass knobs. Inside, walls and earth floors sometimes were plastered and either painted red or whitewashed for brightness. One visitor said they sprinkled the floors with water several times a day to prevent dust. She added that in the center of her room, a large wood post propped up the log ceiling. Instead of the beehive-like domed fireplaces found in Mexico, these fireplaces were built in the English style in an H-shape and back to back so they served adjacent rooms. Three others were U-shaped.

Dishes printed with black designs were used on dining tables inside. One room that archaeologists found may have been a washroom. A nearby deep pit was lined with clay so it would hold water for washroom use. The pit, no doubt, was filled often with water hauled in buckets. In another room, a brass telescope was found. The owner probably took advantage of the height of the outer walls of the fort to study the surrounding landscape and watch for enemies, visitors, or game.

Broken ceramics found at Bent's Old Fort. This type was manufactured in Great Britain, and was popular in America during the 1840s and 1850s.

A Peek Inside

Limestone block walkways covered with thick gravel and sand connected the buildings lining the fort walls. Although it did not rain often, drainage ditches alongside the sidewalk edges kept water from seeping underneath. The drains were filled with sand and covered with wood planks or adobe bricks. In some areas an overhanging roof supported on posts kept rain and sun off the pedestrians.

People walked from their rooms to stores, to warehouses and, outside the fort, to an ice house. Inside one warehouse, the remains of fourteen barrels were found. In another, iron projectile points had been made for the Indian trade from the iron hoops used to hold wooden barrels together. In yet another room was a pit that held several gaming pieces, evidence that the men gambled in their spare time.

The center open space (plaza) was not leveled as neatly as it would be in a military fort. Gravel had been spread over it to keep down the dust and mud. A visitor described this space as "full of noise." She wrote that the clang of horse shoeing, neighing of horses, baying of mules, crying of children, and scolding and fighting of men filled the air. In the middle of the plaza, archaeologists found remains of a pelt press. Holes for three massive posts that supported the press were excavated; the location of the fourth remained unclear. The press was more than 11 feet (3 m) long, larger than most. Its large size indicates that it was used mainly to press buffalo hides rather than beaver.

A well was found inside the first compound built. Over the years additional rooms were added. In the 1840s huge storage pits were dug, probably to help house the 35,000 pounds (16,000 kilograms) of provisions the army stored there.

The largest room in the fort was the wagon room with large doorways. Before it was constructed in 1845, the fort's wagons probably sat under canvas shelters.

The fort's dumps were located between 6 and 40 feet (2 and 12 m) outside the fort walls. Layers of ash and charred material show that trash was burned. The odor of these trash fires must have filled the nostrils of everyone staying there! Cattle and buffalo bones with butchering cuts on them, Indian pottery, and a DuPont black powder canister were still identifiable. Trade beads, clay pipe fragments, and gun parts were numerous.

Household items such as a clock part; pewter

White clay tobacco pipes found at the site of Bent's Old Fort. Tobacco pipe styles changed greatly through time so are a handy tool for dating a site.

spoons; iron pots; brass spigots for draining liquids like vinegar, whiskey, or wine from kegs; iron keys; and padlocks tell of what life was like in the fort. Numerous ceramic fragments show that fragile items such as tableware made it safely down the Santa Fe Trail, only to be broken after arrival.

Dark gray slate fragment bearing an incised design of an Indian moccasin and legging. Paper was scarce, so someone at Bent's Old Fort was doodling on this smooth stone.

Pieces of burned slate still contained some messages. On one, an incised drawing of a Plains Indian leg is clear. The leg is bent and dressed in a tight-fitting pant with fringed buckskin, the foot protected by a fringed moccasin. Incised designs were also found on other slates, one bearing the date 1848.

Two brass wedding rings were recovered from one room, and two others from the trash dump. Were they lost or tossed? We will never know for sure.

Excavating Evidence

For travelers, sighting Bent's Old Fort must have been an exciting moment. They could stop and rest, pick up fresh supplies, and prepare themselves to enter Mexican territory.

Bent's Old Fort played a vital role in the early history of the westward movement. Although most traffic was from businessmen looking for profit from trade between Mexico and the United States, some settlers did go into Mexican territory, obtain land grants, and settle there. After the Mexican War, of course, this land—consisting of Texas, which already had obtained independence from Mexico, today's New Mexico, Arizona, and California—became part of the United States. Then settlers came in larger numbers.

Finding Other Forts

Many forts that were important in the westward movement have been studied by archaeologists. Travelers through what is now the state of Wyoming looked forward to a stop at Fort Laramie. Located on the Laramie River, the fort started as a fur trade post in 1812, was permanently occupied by 1834, and was purchased by the U.S. Army as a base for the protection of travelers on the Oregon Trail in 1849. Archaeological excavations there revealed the location of many buildings. Because of the massive changes to the site over time, few artifacts and structures related to the fur trade era have been located, but the military period is well represented. Today a restored Fort Laramie is operated by the National Park Service.

Fort Hall was an important landmark in what is today's Idaho. It is now located inside the Fort Hall Indian reservation. Careful excavations have been undertaken so as to meet the tribes'

A nineteenth–century painting by W.H. Jackson shows Fort Laramie as it looked about 1845. Located in today's Wyoming, both soldiers and Native Americans regularly visited the fort.

concerns. Constructed in 1834 by a trading company, the fort was a square structure built of logs located along the Snake River. By the 1840s it was an important stop for travelers on the Oregon and Mormon trails and later those rushing to the goldfields. The fort was abandoned in 1856 and destroyed by floods in the 1860s. Its exact location was forgotten, but archaeologists found fort remains intact. Excavations in the 1990s uncovered mud brick foundations, a building inside the fort wall, and artifacts from the various occupations.

Fort Union, a large fur trade post located near the border of today's North Dakota and Montana, represents another early settlement of western territory. The fort was built to last and it did for forty years (1828–1867), the longest of any fur trade post. The ruins survived. After fire destroyed much of the first fort, it was enlarged with four log walls set on stone foundations. Inside were many dwellings, stores, an ice house, a blacksmith shop, a powder magazine, a large administrative building, and warehouses for trade goods brought to the fort. The tens of thousands of artifacts found included bells and mirrors from Germany; beads from Venice, Italy; and marine shells from the Caribbean. Beaver, bear, and buffalo robes were manufactured and stored until they could be sent east as floor coverings, carriage robes, and overcoats. The odors from hundreds of skins, butchering waste, and livestock kept inside the fort must have stunk! Excavations at Fort Union were the largest ever undertaken by the National Park Service, and were followed by reconstruction of some structures. The fort (without the smells) can be visited today.

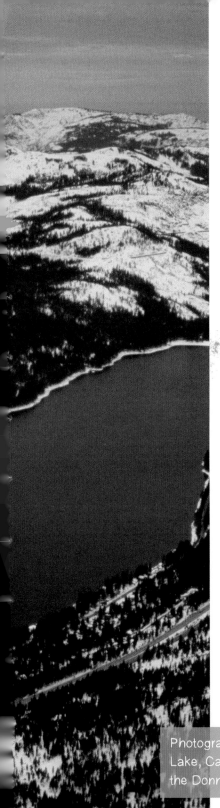

Three
California Bound: The Tragic Donner Party

One of the most famous of westward movement stories is that of a group (party) trapped in the Sierra Nevada Mountains near California. When the survivors were rescued, they talked of eating their dogs, mice, the boiled hides of their oxen—and people who had died.

Photograph of today's Donner Lake, California, named after the Donner party pioneers

Horror at their story swept the nation. Some people today believe members of the party killed one another for food. That was not true. But party members did testify that some were so starved, they ate dead bodies.

A nineteenth-century engraving by an unknown artist shows how members of the Donner party might have huddled together to keep warm during the winter.

What Went Wrong?

Heavy snowfalls began early in the mountains on October 28, 1846, and continued about every two weeks until February. On October 31 the first group of the Donner party reached today's Donner Lake, where they set up camp to wait out the storm. They ended up staying all winter. They lived in three log cabins scattered about half a mile (1 kilometer) apart on a creek.

One cabin built by previous travelers became home to the Breen family. The Kesebergs built a lean-to next to it. The rest of the party built two new cabins. One is called the Murphy cabin, where four families lived; the other was shared by the Graves and Reed families.

The Donner family itself had lagged behind, delayed by a broken wagon axle and the fact that George Donner injured his hand while repairing it. They stopped at what now is called Alder Creek about 5 miles (8 km) northeast of the first camp. Although members of the two groups snowshoed back and forth over the winter, they remained separated. Of the eighty-one people trapped in the two camps, only forty-eight lived to be rescued.

They made at least three attempts to get out; others from the outside also tried to reach them. All efforts failed until February 18, when the first rescue group from the outside arrived at the lake camp. Those who were able to travel—mostly children—left with the rescuers on February 22. A second relief party arrived on March 1. They took seventeen survivors back with them. On the way they were overcome by another snowstorm and had to leave thirteen people in a temporary camp. When a third rescue party found these refugees in mid-March, only ten were still alive, and there were definite signs of cannibalism. The third rescue party continued on to find only ten people left at the lake camp and three at the Alder Creek camp. Because George Donner was dying there, five remained behind to help. In April the last relief group found only one man alive.

The tragic story of the Donner party lives today as an example of how difficult the westward journey could be. Some of the party members' journals were published; their story has been told by others in books, plays, and poems.

Two members of the Donner party, James and Margret Reed, were among the lucky survivors, one of only two families who remained intact.

Early Excavations

Two of the lake campsites were excavated as early as the 1870s. Since then the oldest cabin site has been destroyed by highway construction. The site of the second cabin occupied by the Graves and Reed families was destroyed when a monument was built there in 1909. Recent excavations have studied the Murphy cabin on Donner Lake and the Donner family campsite at Alder Creek.

The Murphy cabin was built against a huge boulder that formed one of its walls. Unable to break through the root mass covering the ground by this large rock, the 1870s excavator did not dig there.

In 1984 archaeologists began work at the site of the Murphy cabin. They took small soil samples from across the site. By analyzing chemicals in the soil, they were able to find the most likely location of the cabin. Excavations then identified occupation layers, along with fire pits, postholes, and artifact clusters. Fire pits were dug by the families along the bottom of the large boulder that formed the cabin's west wall. Water seeping down the wall at different times probably forced them to move the fire pits frequently.

Artifacts relating to the Murphy cabin occupants were found under a layer of rock that had fallen off the boulder. Charred wood, charcoal, and ash from the burning of the cabin also covered the Donner party occupation layers, including a burned log that came from the east wall of the cabin or was a roof support. Burned log walls tend to fall directly down, so lines of thick charcoal and wood ash marked the walls of the cabin. The structure was 18 feet by 25 feet (5 m by 8 m)—a small space for as many as sixteen people!

The cabin's dirt floor contained most of the artifacts. The largest cluster was found in front of the rock wall and the hearth's fire pits. Finds included clothing items, tobacco pipes, and a group of lead shot that was once stored in

Artifacts found at the Donner party lake camp, including charcoal, shot, and a buckle. Notice the small tools (a brush and trowel) used for carefully excavating the site.

a pouch. Firearms of different types were found at all the cabins at the lake camp, including a brass pistol, flintlocks, gun flints, and rifles. The group was well armed!

The presence of women and children is obvious from finds such as glass and ceramic beads from necklaces, a silver-plated dangling earring, a brooch, hairpin, combs, and a small child's shoe heel. An iron key suggests a trunk for storage. A dinner plate decorated with red flowers, brass spoons, a jug handle, and a fragment of a cast-iron cooking pot tell how they cooked and what they put on tables. Excavations in the 1870s uncovered similar decorated dishes, spoons, knives, forks, a darning needle, pins, and glass tumblers at the other lake cabins.

Most of the food bones from the Murphy cabin site were from oxen or cattle, but those of a horse or mule also were found. Bones from two bears were a surprise, as the records mention their eating only one. Cannibalism may have taken place here, but the broken-up burned human bones found were all too small to show any cut marks.

The Donner family lived 5 miles (8 km) away from the lake cabins. One member of this family explained, "We had no time to build a Cabin the Snow came on So Sudden that we had barely time to pitch our tent, and put up a small brush shed . . . covered with pine boughs and then with Rubber coats, Quilts, etc." Another member of the group described "a hut like the Indians Wigwam with an opening at the top." The Donners lived in these shelters all winter. They stood on top of 12-foot-deep (4-m) snow to saw off tree limbs for firewood. One member reported that sometimes they went without fires and meat for days. Then they ate hides and rawhide strings or went hungry. He also wrote that this group did not eat human flesh, but rescue parties reported that they found evidence of cannibalism there.

The Alder Creek campsite is inside today's Tahoe National Forest, but its exact location is a mystery. In the 1920s a visitor to the area identified what he thought was the camp when he spotted 12-foot-tall (4-m) tree stumps probably left by the Donners, who cut them for firewood.

In the 1990s, using metal detectors, archaeologists swept these areas. After mapping in the exact location of each find, they excavated. Artifacts very similar to those from the Murphy cabin site were found, but there was no evidence of shelters, hearths, or storage pits. Perhaps this was where their wagons stood, and the shelters were elsewhere. That the actual campsites remain elusive is not surprising, since they were little more than wigwams and tents.

Archaeologists' Answers

Again the human bone fragments were too small for the archaeologists to be sure that there were no cut marks on some. Other artifacts left by the Donner party were typical of those brought west by most travelers during the 1840s. The fact that fragile items such as ceramic dishes made it that far says that

Archaeologists working at the Donner party lake site are shown slowly removing soil with small trowels.

women protected these reminders of life back home. Information about how the Murphy cabin was built, its size, and the arrangement of the hearth fires inside is useful for understanding how these people endured during that long, cold winter. Perhaps someday the Alder Creek habitation site will be found, giving new information about life inside such flimsy shelters.

The Donner party story remains a symbol of the difficulty of making the trek west. Poor planning and wrong decisions along the way often led to disaster.

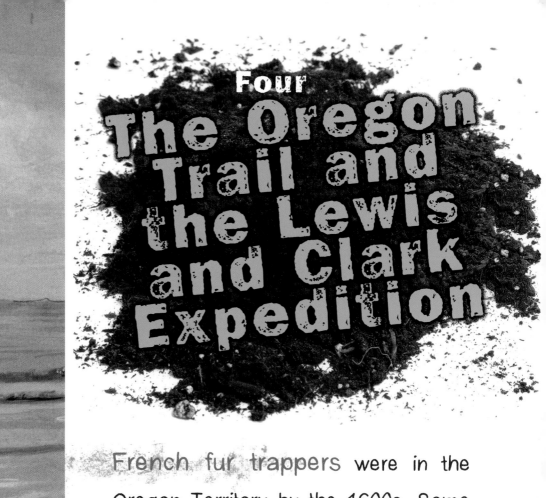

Four
The Oregon Trail and the Lewis and Clark Expedition

French fur trappers were in the Oregon Territory by the 1600s. Some say their word for "hurricane" (*outraging*) was the origin of the territory's name. They called it this because of the violent storms that pounded the mountains.

A painting by an unknown artist showing pioneers traveling the Oregon Trail. The groups spread out for miles during the day but gathered together at night.

English explorer James Cook claimed Oregon for his country. In 1792 American Captain Robert Gray sailed his ship up a river he named Columbia, after his ship. More than ten years later, Lewis and Clark went beyond the boundary of the Louisiana Purchase and reached the Pacific Ocean. They then turned back home—and met fur traders already coming west. People came mostly by boat until the Oregon Trail was established in the 1840s. These included Hawaiians, Russians, Canadians, and various Indian groups from the East, as well as English, Scots, Irishmen, and Americans.

By an agreement drawn up in 1818 and renewed in 1827, the Oregon Territory was shared by Britain and the United States. Finally, in 1846, the border between British Canada and the United States was set at the forty-ninth parallel. Eventually the Oregon Territory south of that became the states of Washington, Idaho, Montana, Wyoming, Utah, and Nevada, as well as British Columbia in Canada.

Until travelers reached today's state of Idaho, the Oregon and California trails followed the same route. In Idaho those bound for today's Oregon bumped their way through the South Pass of the Rocky Mountains, along the Snake River and to the Columbia River, which emptied into the Pacific.

In 1841 a group of settlers made the first attempt at taking wagons to Oregon, but they had to abandon them in the desert near the Great Salt Lake and continue with just their animals. In 1843 the trail finally was established as a wagon road. The federal government built a shortcut between the South Pass through the Rocky Mountains into Snake River country in 1857, making the Oregon Trail the only one that the U.S. government helped finance. Thousands of settlers came over the trail the next year, most traveling 15 miles (24 km) a day from Missouri, a trip that took about six months.

Why travel by lumbering wagon? Why not by ship?

The journey by ship was expensive and could take as long as a year. Most Oregon settlers also came from the midwestern states, so they lived nowhere near the ocean. Loading goods into a wagon and mostly walking to the Oregon Territory made more sense, assuming one could afford the equipment, was healthy, and was prepared for the hardships ahead.

The Lewis and Clark Expedition 1803–1806

A very early trek west was made by the Lewis and Clark expedition. William Clark, Meriwether Lewis, and their troop of thirty-three men traveled mainly by river, stopping about six hundred times to camp overnight. During the first winter they stayed near the Mandan Indians in North Dakota. None of these camps has been found.

A camp farther west at the Lower Portage of the Great Falls in the Missouri River in Montana may have been identified. The travel journals of the expedition speak of spending twelve

Fur Trade Posts

Although the Oregon Trail was not very passable until 1843, fur traders and merchants built posts along it as early as 1810. Places like Fort Astoria, Fort Spokane, and Fort Vancouver have been excavated by archaeologists. Of these three, Fort Vancouver (1829) was the largest and most successful. Built on the Columbia River, it contained buildings for manufacturing, blacksmithing, trading, selling goods, making bread, and dispensing medicines. While Ulysses S. Grant was a storekeeper there, he trusted a friend too much. The friend ran away with Grant's money while Grant's store exploded. The fort was abandoned in 1860 at the beginning of the Civil War. Many years of archaeological excavations have yielded thousands of artifacts, information about the buildings, and led to its reconstruction by the National Park Service. The site can be visited today.

days there while they dried fish and buffalo meat. Archaeologists found the remains of twelve campfires arranged in a line. Radiocarbon dates on a wooden stake and bison bones excavated at the site yielded dates around 1810, plus or minus forty to fifty years, well within the range of the Lewis and Clark expedition.

Their camp near the Pacific Ocean, Fort Clatsop in northwestern Oregon, may also have been identified. Here they stayed for 106 days during the winter of 1805–1806 before turning homeward. Archaeologists in the 1940s and 1950s failed to find evidence of the camp, but more recent work in the 1990s included making detailed maps of the site and using equipment to detect underground features.

Excavations into these features yielded burned bone, charcoal, and a dark earthen pit with a definite right angle, perhaps a building or a square privy pit. One of the artifacts found at the site, a cast-brass bead, was a type that was in use between 1793 and 1820, which suggests that it was left there by the expedition. Also found was a fired musket ball, again suggesting the presence of white men. A blue glass trade bead and another pit feature were found the next year. Soil samples taken across the suspected area of the camp showed that disturbed soils, probably due to fort construction, can be found as deep as 4 feet (1 m) below the surface. More work is planned.

The Mormon Trail

Remote sensing from the air and photography from a slow-moving radio-controlled model airplane has been done to study the remains of the westward movement trails. The Mormon Trail was a route for believers in the Mormon faith to follow west to Utah and return again for fresh supplies. The trail started in Illinois, where many were living, and ended at the Valley of the Salt Lake in Utah. In today's Wyoming, the Mormons crossed to the south side of the Platte River, where they joined the Oregon Trail. In Fort Bridger they left the Oregon Trail and followed the Donner party section of the California Trail to Utah. Researchers have found that the trail was engineered, as it had a drainage system built along it, making it freer of potholes than the others. This made the Mormon Trail a drier, faster route that could be used over and over again. By contrast, photos of the Oregon Trail show frequent fanning out of wagons off the trail to avoid potholes, making the trail wider and slower. Those taking the Oregon Trail were only interested in making the trip once, so no real care was taken. Except for the section engineered by the federal government, it just grew wider. In many places today the parallel ruts are still visible.

Wheels of thousands of wagons on the Oregon Trail left these ruts through a sandstone rock edge near Guernsey, Wyoming.

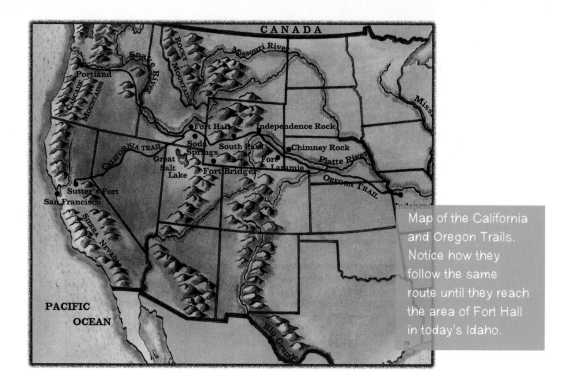

Map of the California and Oregon Trails. Notice how they follow the same route until they reach the area of Fort Hall in today's Idaho.

The Whitman Mission, 1836–1847

Thirty years after the Lewis and Clark expedition visited Oregon, a medical doctor named Marcus Whitman and his bride, Narcissa, along with another missionary couple, Eliza and Henry Spalding, managed to get a wagon across the Rockies, years before the trail was opened. Their trip was made in 1836, when travelers usually left their wagons at Fort Laramie in Wyoming. But because Eliza Spalding was ill, they persisted. This achievement encouraged others to try it, too, and also made it clear that women could endure the difficult journey to Oregon.

The Whitmans established their Christian mission in southeast Oregon, near today's Walla-Walla. Here they worked among the Cayuse Indians, providing medical care and preaching church doctrine. Unfortunately a measles epidemic during which many Cayuse died brought about the Whitmans' deaths. The Indians believed that Dr. Whitman cured white people of measles, but not them. By their customs, that meant the doctor (or shaman, as they called doctors) was dishonest and had to die. Marcus, Narcissa, and twelve others were killed in November 1847, and the mission buildings were burned. The site later was occupied by a new fort, which also burned, and then a house and school that burned in 1872.

Archaeologists investigating the site found the three different layers of ash and charcoal from the fires; this helped them identify each separate occupation on the site. Work began in the 1940s by locating the corners and parts of the walls of the First House, the shelter built by the Whitmans soon after their arrival. The house was built of adobe walls 14 inches (36 centimeters) thick with a cellar for storage underneath. Other finds included a hoe, rotted cottonwood timbers, nails, harness buckles, a pin bent into a fishhook, and glass beads.

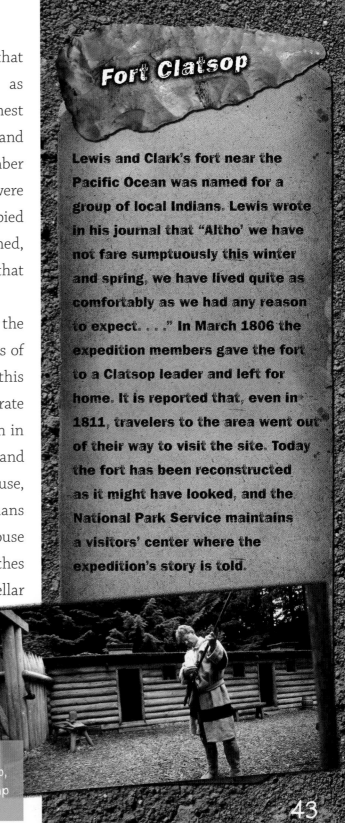

Fort Clatsop

Lewis and Clark's fort near the Pacific Ocean was named for a group of local Indians. Lewis wrote in his journal that "Altho' we have not fare sumptuously this winter and spring, we have lived quite as comfortably as we had any reason to expect. . . ." In March 1806 the expedition members gave the fort to a Clatsop leader and left for home. It is reported that, even in 1811, travelers to the area went out of their way to visit the site. Today the fort has been reconstructed as it might have looked, and the National Park Service maintains a visitors' center where the expedition's story is told.

Photograph of the modern reconstruction of Fort Clatsop, Lewis and Clark's winter camp in Oregon

The earthen roof had collapsed over the remains of the First House.

The Whitmans also built what was called the Emigrant House, where travelers going west were welcome to stay. Little remained of that. Souvenir hunters had dug holes and yanked artifacts out of the earth; some of the soil was carried away to build up the banks of a nearby irrigation ditch. However, archaeologists did find two corners and the outside edge of one wall.

Other sites included that of a gristmill, found by following earthen dikes that led from the original mill pond to a mill race that once carried water to the mill wheel. Archaeologists uncovered pine timbers from the mill wheel platform. A corral for the blacksmith's shop was found to be in the shape of a half circle. Later excavators found more of the blacksmith shop: a clay floor, piles of clinkers (used bits of coal), charcoal, fired clay, slag, and melted iron, evidence of the blacksmith's activities.

Archaeologists working at the Whitman Mission site during the 1940s. This is an example of early historical archaeology.

The Mission House was built when the First House became too small for the Whitmans. It, too, was made of adobe brick, but it contained a living room, bedrooms, a kitchen with a big hearth, a pantry, storeroom, schoolroom, and a meeting room for talks with Native Americans. Built in the shape of a T, its long side measured 102 feet (31 m),

Ceramics found at the Whitman Mission. These were manufactured in Great Britain, shipped over the Atlantic Ocean, across a continent, to be used at the Whitman Mission.

and its shorter side was 60 feet (18 m). Many flakes of plaster and whitewash show that the outside walls had been smoothed with mud plaster and then whitewashed. Again the heavy earthen roof had fallen in during the fire.

Artifacts found at the Mission House included a silver spoon that belonged to Narcissa, charred cloth, a bone shuttle used for weaving, meat hooks, gun parts, a kerosene lamp glass chimney, and, most surprising, several porcelain false teeth! No one knows who owned those. In addition, there were numerous samples of Marcus's rock collection. His hobby was geology, so he collected many kinds of rocks for study.

The site is open to tourists today. Buildings are outlined on the ground so visitors can better understand the layout of this important early pioneer site.

As a result of the tragic misunderstanding that led to the Whitmans' deaths, more American troops came into Oregon. Their presence made emigrants feel safer—and soon they came by the thousands.

Five
Gold-Seekers Rush to the West

When gold was discovered near Sacramento, California, in 1848, gold-seekers flooded in from around the world: Asia, the United States, South America, and Europe. Almost 100,000 people had poured into California by 1850; more than 300,000 came by 1854. In 1848, before gold was discovered, there were fewer than ten Chinese people in California. By 1852 there were at least 20,000 Chinese workers panning for gold.

In this 1871 Currier and Ives lithograph, gold miners are shown using various tools to extract the precious mineral from the earth.

A treaty signed in February 1848 ended the Mexican War. The United States paid Mexico $15 million for all of Mexico's land in North America, including California. Unknown to any of the treaty signers, gold had been discovered the month before, and the rush began by spring. Already by 1850, there were so many Americans in California that it was admitted to the Union as the thirty-first state.

Although most Americans traveled overland by wagon, many chose to come by sea. But there was no direct water route to California. Ships leaving New York City traveled all the way south around the tip of South America, coming very close to the icy continent of Antarctica and running through huge storms along the way. The trip could take a year.

Others elected to take a ship to Panama. There was no Panama Canal then, so the travelers walked, rode canoes, and took wagons for miles overland through hot, dangerous, disease-filled jungles. Then they waited on the Pacific shore for a boat. Weeks, or even months, passed. When a ship finally arrived, the passenger might have to pay as much as a thousand dollars for a berth. And the ships were not very safe. Many sank on their way from Panama to California.

Map of routes followed by boats from the East Coast of North America to San Francisco on the West Coast. The Panama Canal, begun in 1904, certainly was needed!

Those who chose the water route to the gold rush landed in San Francisco. This little Mexican shipping town was transformed into a bustling, messy city as thousands and thousands of people crowded in. When ships arrived in the bay, sometimes the captain and crew joined the passengers and took off for the goldfields! Ships from the United States often were left anchored and empty. Ships that connected with Europe, South and Central America, Australia, New Zealand, Hawaii, and Hong Kong were better at returning home to bring more goods to San Francisco. Millions of tons of cargo were brought by these ships. But San Francisco lacked warehouses to store it all, let alone wharves large enough for off-loading cargoes.

Merchants took action. They filled in the waterfront with sand, rock, garbage, and old ship hulks. They built wharves, and purchased or leased idle anchored ships to pull up onto the mud flats to make stores (storeships), offices, hotels, and even a jail. Some ships were covered over with wood like a building; others were kept as they were. All were hemmed in by networks of piers, wharves, and buildings. People visited these storeships to buy goods; merchants used them as warehouses.

When the gold rush ended about 1854, San Francisco was a developed port for maritime trade, its waterfront vastly changed in just a few years.

Archaeologists Hit Pay Dirt

Today the busy financial district of San Francisco sits on top of the early Mexican and gold rush settlement. Archaeological work in San Francisco's downtown has uncovered several buried storeships. In May 1851 a huge fire had destroyed the storeships. Almost immediately landfill was dumped over them, thus preserving the ship remains and many of the artifacts they held. Among these were the *Niantic* and the *General Harrison*.

Archaeologists from the San Francisco Maritime Museum work inside the hull of the ship *Niantic*, discovered buried under the streets of San Francisco.

The *Niantic* was discovered during development activities in 1978. An emergency excavation recovered part of the remains of the ship and cargo. The ship had been used as a warehouse, holding goods belonging to businessmen of San Francisco, but it also held personal items in what would be called storage lockers today. Most of the warehouse items could be assigned to a specific business. For example, there were bound journals, diaries, lead pencils, brass pen points, ink bottles, and paper being stored by a stationery and office supply business. Each of these items came from a different place: New York City; Concord, Massachusetts; London, England; and Germany. This alone points out the wide range of trade taking place in San Francisco by that time.

In 2001 the *General Harrison* storeship was excavated. The *General Harrison* was in business as a storeship less than a year. Newspaper accounts of the day contain numerous advertisements about sales of goods from this store.

Inside, the storeship held liquor and foodstuffs selected for the San Francisco market and sold by auction from the ship. This included wine and beer from many different countries, and food like beans, dried fruits, and barley from Chile. In fact, documentary research shows that both the *Niantic* and the *General Harrison* storeships were owned by Chileans! People from many different nations had rushed in, some to hunt for gold, others to supply those who came. And the suppliers made the most money.

More Discoveries

Many ships were recycled. Using floats and lines passed under the keel of a vessel, older, less useful ships had been hauled up on the beach at high tide. During low tide the ships were dismantled. Useful ship objects such as anchors, rigging, and pumps were set aside for resale. Nails, spikes, and other fasteners were sold for scrap. Good timber probably was reused in new ships, while older rotted wood was cut up to feed the fires of nearby factories. In this manner, between 1854 and 1859, more than two hundred ships disappeared. Documentary research shows that much of this work was done by Chinese immigrants.

Clusters of artifacts uncovered by archaeologists under the San Francisco streets may represent these work areas. In fact, a large iron bar found with a chisel-like tip probably was used by Chinese workers to pry open the vessel timbers. Builders' marks were common on wood, incised numbers that indicated the order in which the ship originally was put together. Metal artifacts left behind included copper sheathing, chain links, and iron fittings for masts. By studying these remains, the archaeologists were able to identify the sizes of ships being dismantled, dates of manufacture, use, abandonment, and the types of fittings used.

The archaeological finds show that this was an organized, careful process. The fact that they recycled ship hulks shows that Californians knew they were isolated by 3,000 miles (5,000 km) from the East Coast by land and 14,000 miles (23,000 km) by ocean. They could not—and did not—waste much!

Pioneers who traveled the Oregon Trail sometimes left their names or initials on what is now known as "Register Cliff" at the Green River Crossing near Guernsey, Wyoming.

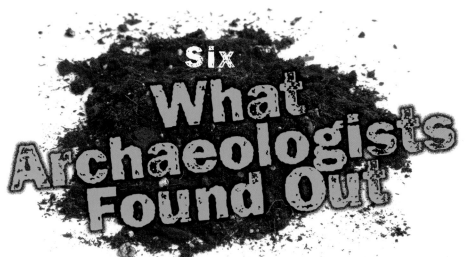

Six
What Archaeologists Found Out

Movements into today's western states began early, with the Spanish claiming much of what is now the United States. The British claimed the Oregon Territory, and the French and Spanish held the Louisiana Territory. Because these various ownerships complicated the westward movement of U.S. citizens, claims of these different nations had to be settled through war and treaties. People from many other nations also came, making the American West a place where various cultures mixed together early on.

Archaeologists have studied these early movements and have come to understand life at fur posts, forts, and missions. They have pieced together evidence of how the trails developed and of disasters that occurred as explorers, fur trappers, fur traders, and settlers moved westward. Overland travel by wagon and foot eventually ended with the building of the Transcontinental Railroad, completed in 1869. Archaeology has shown how people moving west adapted and survived in environments and among Native peoples that were strange, alien, and hostile. The movement of people westward was part of a process that had been going on for three hundred years.

Settlers in the West quickly set up settlements such as cities, mining towns, small farming villages, and ranches. Archaeologists also are busy studying these settlements to see what happened once travelers reached their destinations.

1540–1542 Coronado establishes Spanish claim to much of the West.

1598 First Spanish/Mexican permanent settlement in land Coronado explored.

1792 Americans sail up Columbia River, laying claim to Oregon.

1803 Louisiana Territory purchased from Napoleon, leader of France.

1803–1806 Lewis and Clark expedition explores land west of Saint Louis.

1821 Mexico wins independence from Spain; gains much of today's Southwest. General date for beginning of Santa Fe Trail as Mexico opens for trade.

1828 Fort Union built near today's North Dakota and Montana border; occupied until 1867. Example of large busy fort built by early westward-moving businessmen.

1829 Fort Vancouver replaces 1824 fort; abandoned in 1860.

1830–1842 Indians east of Mississippi forced to give up lands; many move west.

1830 Western part of Oregon Trail opened.

1833 Bent's Old Fort begun; blown up in 1849; Bent's New Fort built.

1834 Fort Hall built in today's Idaho. First missionaries in Oregon.

1835–1840 Fur trade in Rockies ends.

1836 Texas wins independence from Mexico.
Whitmans begin mission in Oregon.

1841 Overland migration to California begins.

1842–1843 Large-scale migration to Oregon.

1845 Texas gets statehood.

1846–1847 Donner party snowbound in Sierra Nevada Mountains on the way to California.

1847 Mormons reach Utah.
Cayuse Indians kill the Whitmans.

1848 First Chinese arrive in California.
End of Mexican War; United States gains vast lands.
Gold discovered in California.

1849–1851 San Francisco develops even more as an important port.

1850 California granted statehood.

adobe—Clay mixed with straw used to make sun-dried bricks.

berth—Place to sleep on a ship.

bison—Correct name for the American buffalo.

black powder—Explosive used in guns.

cannibalism—Act of eating others of one's own kind.

cutlass—Short curving sword with one sharp edge.

dike—Ditch or watercourse, or a bank of earth piled up while digging a ditch.

forty-ninth parallel—Artificial line shown on maps and globes located 49 degrees north of the equator.

geology—Study of the earth's crust, including individual rocks and fossils.

keel—Main timber extending the entire length of a boat/ship.

keg—Small barrel for holding liquids, usually less than 10 gallons (38 liters); also used for nails and many other items.

kerosene—Rhin oil made from coal or oil used in lamps, stoves, and engines.

lean-to—Structure supported by a wall, having a single sloping roof and enclosed for living or storage.

limestone—Rock originally formed underwater and hardened; used for building.

Louisiana Territory—Land purchased from France in 1803; extended from the Gulf of Mexico to Canada and from the Mississippi River to the Rocky Mountains.

Mountain Men—Fur trappers and traders in the Rocky Mountains during the 1820s and 1830s who helped open up that territory.

pedestrian—Someone walking; traveling on foot.

pelt press—Device for flattening furs and tying them in bundles for easier shipping.

pike—Weapon with a metal spearhead on the end of a long wooden shaft.

powder flask—Small flat container for gunpowder.

projectile point—Sharp stone or metal blade made by Indians and mounted on the end of a weapon.

pueblo—Village of flat-roofed adobe structures arranged in terraces; type built by Indians in the American Southwest.

remote sensing—Using various electronic instruments to locate buried features or metal artifacts.

rigging—Ropes used to support ships' masts or to work the sails.

sheathing—Protective cover on a ship's hull or a building.

siege—Surrounding a settlement or fort for a time in order to conquer it.

slag—Waste material from working with metal.

slate—Type of rock so smooth it can be used for drawing or writing.

spigot—Type of faucet inserted into a barrel (keg).

tannery—Place where leather is made from hides.

weaving shuttle—Instrument that carries thread back and forth on a loom.

whetstones—Rough stones used to sharpen metal edges.

Books

Broida, Marian. *Projects About Nineteenth-Century Chinese Immigrants*. New York: Marshall Cavendish, 2006.

Fradin, Dennis. *The Lewis and Clark Expedition*. New York: Marshall Cavendish, 2008.

Harness, Cheryl. *The Tragic Tale of Narcissa Whitman and a Faithful History of the Oregon Trail*. Washington, DC: National Geographic, 2006.

Olson, Tod. *How to Get Rich in the California Gold Rush: An Adventurer's Guide to the Fabulous Riches Discovered in 1848*. Washington, DC: National Geographic, 2008.

Websites

"American West"
www.americanwest.com/trails

California Ho! By the Sea
www.shipofgold.com/goldrush.html

Coronado Slept Here: Discovering a Campsite in Texas
www.psi.edu/coronado/campsite.html

Gold Rush Fun Fact: To California via Antarctica
www.isu.edu/~trinmich/funfacts.html

Books and Articles

Archaeological Institute of America. "Searching for Lewis & Clark," by Jessica E. Saraceni. In *Newsbriefs*, vol. 51 no. 1, January/February 1998.

Bacon, Melvin, and Daniel Blegen. *Bent's Fort, Crossroads of Cultures on the Santa Fe Trail*. Brookfield, CT: The Millbrook Press, 1995.

Coit, Margaret L., and Editors of *Life. The Sweep Westward. Life History of United States* series, edited by Henry F. Graff. vol. 4, 1829–1849. New York: Time Incorporated, 1963.

Comer, Douglas C. *Webs of Significance, Trails From Above*. Silver Spring, MD: Cultural Resource Management, National Park Service's Applied Archeology Center, 2007.

Dary, David. *The Santa Fe Trail: Its History, Legends, and Lore*. New York: Alfred A. Knopf, 2000.

Delgado, James P. "The Archaeology of San Francisco's Gold Rush Waterfront, 1849–1851: Building a New Model of the 19th century Pacific Rim Maritime Frontier." Talk presented at SHA meetings, January 2008.

Drumm, Stella A., ed. *Down the Santa Fe Trail and Into Mexico: The Diary of Susan Shelby Magoffin 1846–1847*. New Haven, CT: Yale University Press, 1926.

Haecker, Charles, National Park Service scientist, SHA talk, January 2008. Trace element analysis; conclusions about bolt heads tested for lead isotope ratios.

Hardesty, Donald L. *The Archaeology of the Donner Party*. Reno, NV: University of Nevada Press, 1997.

Kinder, Gary. *Ship of Gold in the Deep Blue Sea*. New York: The Atlantic Monthly Press, 1998.

Kirk, Ruth, and Richard D. Daugherty. *Archaeology in Washington*. Seattle, WA: University of Washington Press, 2007.

Matzko, John. *Reconstructing Fort Union*. Lincoln, NE: University of Nebraska Press, 2001.

Moore, Jackson W. Jr. *Bent's Old Fort: An Archaeological Study*. Denver, CO: State Historical Society of Colorado, 1973.

Pastron, Allen G., and James P. Delgado. "Archaeological Investigations of a Mid-19th-century Shipbreaking Yard, San Francisco, California." In *Historical Archaeology*, vol. 25 no. 3 (1991): 61–77.

Ronda, James P., and Nancy Tystad Koupal, eds. *Finding Lewis & Clark, Old Trails, New Directions*. Pierre, SD: South Dakota Historical Society Press, 2004.

Vierra, Bradley J. *A Sixteenth-Century Spanish Campsite in the Tiguex Province*. Santa Fe, NM: Laboratory of Anthropology Note No. 475, 1989. Report on excavations.

Walker, Danny N., ed. *Archeology at the Fort Laramie Quartermaster Dump Area, 1994–1996*. Denver, CO: Cultural Resource Selections, Intermountain Region, National Park Service, no. 13, 1998.

Wylie, Alison. "Invented Lands/Discovered Pasts: The Westward Expansion of Myth and History." In *Historical Archaeology*, vol. 27 no. 4 (1993): 1–19.

Websites

Archaeological Institute of America. "Digging San Francisco." Interview with Allen Pastron about his work there.
www.archaeology.org/online/interviews/pastron.html

Daniel M. Rosen. "The Donner Party."
www.donnerpartydiary.com/

Fort Hall: Test Excavations at Fort Hall, Idaho, Summary Results; Fort Hall time line.
www.forthall.net/broadsheet

National Park Service. "Lewis and Clark National Historical Park, Overview of Archaeological Exploration, 1957-58; 1990s. Process of Discovery: Archaeological Excavations at Fort Clatsop."
www.nps.gov/lewi/historyculture/arch5758-overview.htm

Melissa O'Meara, *Bee* newspaper graphic assistant compiler.
www.goldridge08.com/goldrushtimeline.htm

PBS-The West. Francisco Vazquez de Coronado, 1510–1554.
www.pbs.org/weta/thewest/people/a_c/coronado.htm

To California via Antarctica, June 2008. Idaho State University.
http://www.isu.edu/~trinmich/funfacts.html

Trails West. "The Oregon Trail." Source of information about federal government building shortcut on Oregon trail.
www.tngenweb.org/tnletters/usa-west.htm

About the Author

Lois Miner Huey is a historical archaeologist working for the State of New York. She has published many articles about history and archaeology in kids' magazines as well as a book biography of the Mohawk Indian woman, Molly Brant. She and her archaeologist husband live near Albany, New York, in an old house with four affectionate cats.

WITHDRAWN